This Book Belongs To:

____

SILLY CORGI: DOGS DON'T EAT PIZZA!

SILLY CORGI: DOGS DON'T EAT PIZZA!

Written By Neisha Lopez

Illustrated By Aisha Haider

This book was written to help educate children about table foods that can be harmful to dogs, while giving them a healthy option as well. Pet care is so important for the health and longevity of your furry friend.

My hope is to raise awareness among children and adults about what foods are safe and unsafe for dogs to eat.

Cornelius the Corgi was my furry friend. He was the best dog ever. Unfortunately, he developed Evan's Syndrome at just shy of three years old. Evan's Syndrome can randomly develop in dogs by genetic predisposition. A secondary cause can be due to infections, vaccinations, medications, or exposure to toxins. When we initially took him to the emergency vet, we were asked by the vet if he had been exposed to rat poison. He had not. They then asked if he had eaten onions or garlic. To our knowledge, he had not, but this did make us question every food that we had ever fed him. I realized that a lot of pet owners may not be aware of how harmful some table foods can be for dogs. I decided to write this book in his honor.

The last page has a list of recommended healthy foods and a list of harmful foods. The page can be cut out and used as a quick reference guide.

Follow the adventures of a curious Corgi named Cornelius who would love nothing more than to eat the same meals and treats that his humans eat.

But as Cornelius soon discovers, there are human foods that can be very dangerous for dogs.

Through whimsical illustrations and storytelling, children will learn the important lessons about human foods dogs can safely eat, and which foods they can not.

Cornelius the Corgi was so excited to find his forever home.

The first thing Cornelius did was run outside and play in the grass. He rolled around in the grass, and then he basked in the sun.

This fun adventure made Cornelius very hungry.

It was time for him to have dinner. He went to his bowl, and he ate his yummy kibble. However, he could also smell something else.

As his family sat around the dinner table, Cornelius sniffed the yummy food. Silly Corgi, dogs don't eat pizza!
Pizza has pepperoni and pepperoni is not safe for dogs to eat.

What treat can we give him instead?
Let's give him a carrot. Carrots are good for dogs.
Cornelius loved the healthy carrot.

The next day, Cornelius was so excited to go to the park.

At the park he played fetch with his ball, and he learned
how to catch a frisbee. Cornelius also met a lot of new
dog friends.

Of course this new adventure made Cornelius very
hungry.

He ran up to his family as they shared a piece of chocolate. Cornelius sniffed the chocolate.

Silly Corgi, dogs don't eat Chocolate!

Chocolate is very dangerous for dogs to eat.

What treat can we give him instead?

Let's give him a piece of watermelon. Watermelon is a great treat for dogs especially on a hot Summer day.

Cornelius really enjoyed the healthy piece of watermelon.

The next morning, Cornelius woke up with a lot of energy. He ran up and down the stairs and he played with his toys.

This made Cornelius very hungry.

His family was eating breakfast and he sniffed the bacon on the table.

Silly Corgi, dogs don't eat bacon!

Bacon is not safe for dogs to eat!

What can we give him instead?

Let's give him some strawberries. **Strawberries** are a great treat for dogs!

Cornelius just loved the strawberries and he even wanted seconds.

Cornelius was so excited for his first picnic. He enjoyed
running around and getting wet in the sprinklers.

This made Cornelius very hungry.

He sniffed the food on the picnic table. It was a hamburger.

Silly Corgi, dogs don't eat Hamburgers!

Hamburgers can have onions on them, and onions are not safe for dogs to eat.

What can we give him instead?

Let's give him a some blueberries. Blueberries are a great treat for dogs.

Cornelius loved the blueberries, but most of all, he loved to throw them in the air to catch them, then eat them.

Cornelius was so excited to go to his first parade.

He observed the parade passing by as someone tossed candy to the spectators.

This made Cornelius very curious.

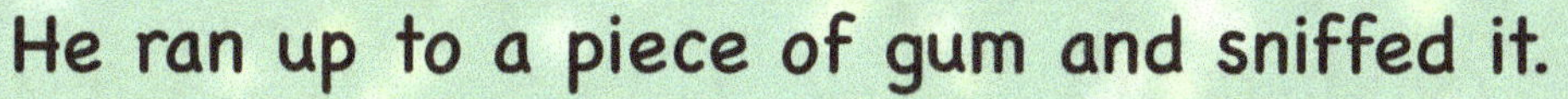

He ran up to a piece of gum and sniffed it.

Silly Corgi, dogs don't eat Gum!

Gum is very dangerous for dogs to eat.

What can we give him instead?

Let's give him a piece of apple (without the seeds).
Dogs can have slices of apples.

Cornelius ate the apple and continued to enjoy the parade.

On this day, Cornelius went on his first road trip. He was so excited!

He looked out the window at all of the cars and the scenery.

This made Cornelius very happy!

When it came time for snacks. Cornelius focused on the grapes.

Silly Corgi, dogs don't eat grapes!

Grapes are very dangerous for dogs to eat.

What can we give him instead?

Let's give him a piece of banana. Dogs can have bananas.

Cornelius loved the banana.

Cornelius the Corgi is enjoying his new home. He's a very curious puppy. He loves to explore around his home and his backyard.

He loves his family and is so grateful to them for making sure he eats healthy and safe treats.

Safe   Unsafe

Safe	Unsafe
Apples (no seeds)	Apple seeds
Asparagus	Bacon
Bananas	Caffeine
Blackberries	Candy
Blueberries	Chives
Broccoli	Chocolate
Cantalope	Coffee
Carrots	Dark Chocolate
Celery	Fat Trimmings
Cranberries	Garlic
Cucumbers	Grapes
Eggs	Gum
Kiwi	Mushrooms
Mango	Nuts
Pears	Onions
Peas	Prosciutto
Pineapple	Raisins
Raspberries	Rhubarb
Strawberries	Tea
Watermelon	Xylitol

This list is provided as a quick reference and has a list of safe foods that my pets have eaten. I encourage you to conduct your own research or speak to your Veterinarian to make informed decisions for your pet.

About The Author ✍️

Neisha Romo Lopez was born and raised in Douglas, Arizona. She currently lives in Tempe, Arizona with her husband Salvador. They have a daughter, Kassandra Lopez and a son, Ignacio Lopez. Neisha's book idea was inspired by Corgi Cornelius. Cornelius was at the emergency vet several times. While there, she observed that many pet owners struggled to afford emergency veterinary care. This realization motivated her to write a book in Cornelius's honor who sadly passed away from Evan's Syndrome. She decided to start an emergency vet fund to help families with their emergency vet bills.

A portion of "Silly Corgi, Dog's Don't Eat Pizza!" will be donated to the Cornelius Emergency Vet Fund, helping pet owners afford essential emergency care for their pets.

www.corneliusemergencyvetfund.com